Mel Bay Presents

Stéphane GRAPPELLI

GYPSY JAZZ VIOLIN

by Tim Kliphuis

Cover sketch of Grappelli by Merryl Jaye. All Rights Reserved. Used by Permission.
For more information contact: Jayepaint@aol.com

CD contents

1 Tuning note A = 440 hz	12 Lick # 11	23 Backing for Improvisation No. 3
2 Lick # 1	13 Lick # 12	24 Backing for Improvisation No. 4
3 Lick # 2	14 Lick # 13	25 Backing for Improvisation No. 5
4 Lick # 3	15 Lick # 14	26 Backing for Improvisation No. 6
5 Lick # 4	16 Lick # 15	27 Blues in C Improvisation
6 Lick # 5	17 Lick # 16	28 Two Five Stomp Improvisation
7 Lick # 6	18 C major chord	29 Improvisation No. 2 Example
8 Lick # 7	19 A minor chord	30 Improvisation No. 3 Example
9 Lick # 8	20 Backing for Blues in C	31 Improvisation No. 4 Example
10 Lick # 9	21 Backing for Two Five Stomp	32 Improvisation No. 5 Example
11 Lick # 10	22 Backing for Improvisation No. 2	33 Improvisation No. 6 Example

1 2 3 4 5 6 7 8 9 0

Visit us on the Web at www.melbay.com — E-mail us at email@melbay.com

CONTENTS

INTRODUCTION

This book is for any violinist or fiddler of classical, jazz or folk background who wants to learn the famous Stéphane Grappelli Gypsy Jazz style. Good reading ability as well as a basic command of the instrument are recommended.

I have tried to present the information step by step, in easy chunks. You will find theory, exercises and licks as you go. The index on page 73 tells you where to find a certain term or technique if you want it explained. And if you have any other questions about this book, don't hesitate to get in touch.

Everything comes together in the Tunes section. Here, Grappelli's solos are used to discuss tunes, chords, licks and improvisation. Feel free to move back and forth between chapters as they all interrelate. If you haven't improvised before, it is best to follow the general order.

On the CD you will find licks to illustrate certain examples in the book. There are also 9 playalong tracks covering chords and tunes. They feature a rhythm section of guitar and bass, Grappelli's favorite lineup. Samples of Gypsy Jazz violin soloing can be found on separate tracks. Get your hands on the 6 transcribed Grappelli recordings in this book. All the info is there. And if you want to listen to more classic jazz violin, see the discography for suggestions.

As soon as you have the basics sorted out, find a group to work on some tunes. There are loads of fiddlers, guitarists, mandolinists and bassists out there, who are all interested in this music. The Gypsy Jazz scene is well represented worldwide and is growing every day. You will find web groups, jam nights at cafés, festivals and workshops.

Get out there, find other string players and start jamming. Enjoy!

Tim Kliphuis, The Netherlands, 2008

ABOUT THE AUTHOR

Dutchman Tim Kliphuis, one of the world's finest jazz violinists, takes the style of Stéphane Grappelli forward by fusing it with Classical and Folk music. Since the start of his solo career in 2004, Kliphuis has performed with Bucky Pizzarelli, Martin Taylor, Bob Wilber, Fapy Lafertin, Angelo Debarre and Stochelo Rosenberg, and also Jay Ungar and Frankie Gavin. He performs internationally at venues ranging from jazz clubs to Folk festivals and Classical concert halls, including North Sea and Edinburgh Jazz Festival, Djangofests in the States, Ronnie Scott's London, Richard Strauss Festival and Concertgebouw Amsterdam. His CD *The Grappelli Tribute* (2005) was released to rave reviews, followed by *Swingin' Through the Classics* (2007) and *Live in Glasgow* (2007) and *Counterpoint Swing* (2008). Tim is an experienced teacher of jazz violin with workshops all over the world, and many of his students are performers in their own right.

www.timkliphuis.com
www.myspace.com/timkliphuis

Photographer: Marco Borggreve

ACKNOWLEDGEMENTS

My sincere thanks go out to a number of people without whom this book would never have been written:

To Ferdinand Povel for helping me shape my ideas on jazz theory and time, Peter Anick for starting a discussion on how to teach violinists the Grappelli style, and Len Skeat for kick-starting my solo career by putting a UK band together and getting it on the road, in the process telling many great Grappelli stories.

To William Bay for taking on the book, Charles Alexander of Jazzwise UK for his valuable advice, my students Marielle and Janet for their feedback and Janneke for her continuing support and expertise.

To the Grappelli Estate in the persons of Joseph Oldenhove and Eveline Grappelli, for their approval of this project.

And last but not least - to Stéphane Grappelli himself, who opened my ears to the joy and freedom of jazz improvisation on the violin.

STÉPHANE GRAPPELLI

Born in 1908, Stéphane Grappelli went through several dance bands playing piano, violin and saxophone before he met gypsy guitarist Django Reinhardt, who was then better known for his banjo playing. The two had an instant rapport and with the backing of Joseph Reinhardt, Roger Chaput (guitars) and Louis Vola (bass) they formed the Quintette of the Hot Club of France in 1934.

Sporting an unconventional jazz line-up of strings only, the Quintette soon burst onto the scene, recording countless albums and playing all over Europe and the UK. Grappelli was the ideal sideman, communicating with agents and making sure Django turned up at the gig (he might be fishing or playing billiards in the café), but Reinhardt was the star of the group. All recordings from this period show Stéphane shaping his talent and rapidly becoming an all-round jazz musician.

World War II found Reinhardt in Paris and Grappelli in London. Grappelli stayed, performing mostly with pianists George Shearing and Alan Clare. In 1946, the Quintette were reunited, resulting in a famed recording of the Marseillaise, but they never equalled their prewar success. Less than ten years later, Django had passed away and Stéphane was playing Parisian hotel lobbies for a living, with every now and then a performance at Ronnie Scott's, an occasional jazz festival and notably Newport Jazz (USA).

Grappelli's renaissance came in 1973. After he played the Edinburgh Jazz Festival with Alan Clare, the Hot Club of London featured him at big festivals such as the Cambridge Folk Festival, followed by TV shows and festivals in the UK. Not only was he an instant hit with all the old Hot Club fans, but he also captivated huge classical and folk audiences. Stéphane Grappelli had matured into a fabulous jazz player with total freedom on his instrument.

Right up until his death in 1997, he recorded and performed tirelessly all over the world, in groups with such artists as Bucky Pizzarelli and Martin Taylor, but he also worked with a host of greats including Joe Pass, Oscar Peterson, Dizzy Gillespie, Paul Simon and Lord Yehudi Menuhin.

His classical tuition at the Paris Conservatoire and later, during the war years, with concert violinist Alfredo Campoli in England, combined with his ear for melody and his faultless time to make him the most recorded jazz artist in history: Stéphane Grappelli, the man who gave swing to the violin.

GETTING READY

Here are a few tips how to handle your violin the right way, so that it will give you the best possible sound in return. Incidentally, when I say violin I mean fiddle just as well. These are just two different terms for the same instrument. Whether you are a bluegrass fiddler or a classical violinist, just check the following tips before you start.

TUNING

Tune your A string to the tuning note on track number 1 of the playalong CD. It is advisable to keep your instrument in tune when practising at home, otherwise you will have a hard time staying in tune on a gig or jam session.

Tune the other strings to the A making sure that the fifths are nice and tight. If not, your G string will be too low and your E too high. To hear what I mean, check the E and G to the same notes on a (tuned) piano.

STRINGS

Every type of string has its advantages and disadvantages. Gut strings make a warm, classical sound but you might find harmonics difficult to play. Metal strings might sound too harsh. Find strings to suit your violin. You don't need a lot of power - a light, clear sound is more important. I started using John Pearse's Artiste strings because they have good tuning stability and the harmonics are easy to play. Check them out.

STANCE

When you hold the violin under your chin, keep the scroll on the same level as the chinrest. The alignment of the violin should be more or less horizontal. Many players hold the instrument pointing down which makes the bow attack less powerful (as the bow slides away from the bridge). And a good bow attack is necessary, as you will see later in the book.

Keep both feet on the ground, slightly apart, where your right foot is directly below the right shoulder. Stand relaxed and do not lock your knees. If you are tense, lean against a door practicing for a while. This will relax your general stance.

BOW

Wind your bow until the space between wood and hair is the same as the width of the stick. The natural curve in the middle should still be there. If your bow is too tight it will be too jumpy and affect your timing.

Use a little rosin every two days. Don't overdo it, it shouldn't come off in clouds when playing. When you rosin up your bow, do it slowly from top to bottom. The hair has little 'teeth' which you don't want to damage, as that will affect the bow's attack.

Grip your bow at the frog, not higher up. Your thumb should touch the frog. Drape your fingers over the bow, keeping middle and ring finger slightly together, and then put the little finger on top of the bow, keeping it curved instead of straight.

RIGHT ELBOW

Holding your bowing elbow too high or too low can hamper your playing. Play the open strings G-D-A-E and back, following them with your right elbow and make sure you feel comfortable. As a rule, the right hand should not be at an angle, but should rather feel as the continuation of your arm. That leaves the wrist in a neutral position, allowing the muscles and tendons to relax.

BRIDGE

The bridge is the bit of wood that holds the strings up and conveys their sound onto the top of the violin. It should be reasonably straight and stand at a 90 degree angle. It normally is aligned between the two dashes of the f-holes. If you are unsure whether it is allright, go to any violinmaker and they will set it for you.

NOTATION

Here is a complete list of musical symbols used in this book, with their usage and names. Classical players will be more familiar with the first half, whereas jazz and folk players will have come across the second half more often. Have a quick read through and use it as a reference for the following chapters.

Down bow
Bow in the direction of the tip (away from your bowing hand)

Up bow
Bow in the direction of the frog (towards your bowing hand)

Slur
Use one bow to play more than one note

Short note
Make the note shorter than its value by cutting it off from its following note, without leaving the string

Long note
Play the note for its full value so that it connects to the following note

Accent
Give the beginning of a note a kick by applying pressure and then release when starting to bow it

Stretch
The fourth finger of the left hand is extended to play a note just out of position, while the hand remains in place

Left hand pizzicato
Pluck an open string with third or fourth finger of the left hand, without touching the string with the bow

Harmonic
Play a finger without pressing it down, resting it very lightly on the string

Slide
Approach a note from below, moving the finger up

Fall
Let the note drop down after hitting it, moving the finger downwards

Push
Play two notes with one finger, sliding up a semitone to the new note

Pull
Play two notes with one finger, sliding down to the new note

Chop
Hit the string from the air near the frog of the bow, creating very short and punchy notes

Ghost notes
Bow all the notes but make no sound on the ones between brackets, by releasing bow pressure

All the bars in this book are 4/4 measure. Keys are indicated by the number of sharps and flats directly at the start of the bar. Incidental sharps and flats hold for the duration of the bar, in a certain octave.

A LITTLE THEORY

Gypsy Jazz relies heavily on the repertoire of the old Hot Club Quintette of France, with Django Reinhardt and Stéphane Grappelli originals such as Minor Swing, Daphne, Swing '39 and Nuages. But like any other jazz group, the Quintette also recorded countless American swing jazz standards, including I Can't Give You Anything But Love, Sweet Georgia Brown, Limehouse Blues and Honeysuckle Rose.

A tune always has a *theme*, or *head*, which is the melody accompanied by chords (the *chord progression*). Most tunes are 12, 16 or 32 bars in length (a *chorus*). After playing the head once, improvisation starts, following the chord progression of the tune. This is done on repeated choruses, until either the head is played again or someone gives a cue. The song ends on the final bar of the last chorus.

Chords

We will start by looking at how chords work. First, find out the *key* or *tonic* chord of a song by checking the final bar and by counting the number of sharps or flats at the start. For a listing of common Gypsy Jazz keys and their sharps and flats check the end of the Chord Practice chapter, page 29.

Take the key of C major (no sharps, no flats). The tonic chord, C, looks like this:

The tonic chord is an end, a base, and it doesn't lead anywhere else. It is the root of the song, called *I* (one). But to arrive there, we need another chord, called the *dominant* chord, G^7. It is a fifth above the tonic, so we call it the *V* (five). I and V are *steps* in the key of C.

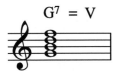 

The V has an extra note added, **f**, which is the *seventh* or 7, so we are really talking about a *dominant 7* chord. It strengthens the urge to come back to the I, which prompted one of my students to call it the "comeback chord". The 7 of the V is an extra *leading* note into the I.

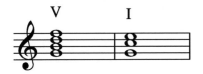 

(I have juggled the notes of the I around to make a *better* voicing. It is still the same three note chord.) In classical music, an extra chord was added to add to the suspense, which is called the *subdominant* chord, or *IV* (four).

Together, the three chords IV-V-I form a *cadence*. The cadence is the basis of nearly all music.

(Again, I have juggled the notes around to accommodate the voicing.) In jazz, however, the sequence IV-V-I constricted bass players when they started to play four notes to the bar. Here is a possible bassline, notated in the treble clef but sounding two octaves down:

There aren't enough steps from IV to V to make a nice walking line. That is why the IV-V evolved into II-V, giving the bassist more freedom of movement:

Let's look at the II. It is a minor chord with a subdominant function. Here, as with the V, the 7 is added. This makes the II look more like the IV (compare them, all the notes of the IV are now in the II):

The II's 7 (**c**) is an extra leading note into V, making the II a bit like a 'minor' dominant for V, which strengthens the direction of the cadence: II leads to V and V leads to I.

We will use the I, IV and V steps in the Blues, and the II-V-I cadence in most other tunes (see Improvisation and Tunes sections).

As you will see in the next chapter, chords are closely linked to *scales*. In minor keys, gypsy jazz uses the *harmonic minor* scale as a basis. The harmonic minor scale borrows its seventh note from the corresponding major scale. This note is called, not surprisingly, *major 7*. Here is the harmonic scale of A minor, where the seventh note (**g♯**) is taken from A major:

Notice that there is a big three-semitone gap between **f** (the 6) and **g♯** (major 7). This gives the scale a kind of gypsy flavor. This gap has consequences for the minor jazz cadence. Here is the I in Am:

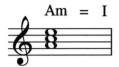 

Next is the V. In minor, usually an extra note is added on top of the 7. It is the 9, and you can see that it is the **f**, which in combination with the **g♯** makes the dominant even more poignant. The name for this type of dominant chord is *flat 9*.

And below is the II. It is no longer just a minor 7 chord. Its 5 (the **f** again!) is flat compared to the root, the **b**. The name for this chord is *minor 7 flat 5*, or *half diminished*.

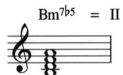 

This is what the full minor cadence looks like (I have left out the root of V because of voicing):

Check out the discussion of the Am improvisation on page 44 for steps I, IV and V in a minor chorus, to experience the sound of the harmonic minor scale and to see the use of the flat nine dominant chord.

That's all for now concerning chord theory. Having mastered chord steps I, II, IV and V you can deal with most of the gypsy jazz repertoire. The next chapter shows how to fit notes to the steps by using one scale to fit them all.

Scales

When I started on this book I decided not to spend too much time talking about scales. Especially if you are new to jazz, they seem very complicated. They have fancy names and notes that don't make sense. The funny thing is, everything you play can be analyzed in terms of scales, but you don't have to think about them very much at all!

In gypsy jazz, think in major or minor. Everything else follows from that. Let's look at the major scale of C.

As you see, the eighth note brings us back to **c**. A scale has seven different notes, or steps. This is where the steps shown in last chapter come in: their root notes correspond with the steps of the scale. Here are I, II, IV and V again (VI will be discussed in the Tunes section; III and VII are beyond the scope of this book). Remember the II and V have an added 7:

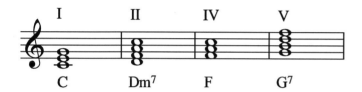

In fact, all the chord notes are scale notes: these are *diatonic* chords. That means you can use one scale playing over all the chords, without a clash. Try it:

Of course, some notes sound better than others. The secret is to play chord notes on the beats, and not worry about the off-beat notes. Here is a diatonic Grappelli example of what I mean:

The notes played on the beats (four beats to a bar) are **c**, **e**, **a** and **b**. The **a** and **b** are not strictly in the chord of C but they are common additions. Try the following chords on the piano - they contain these two additions to the C major triad and a third, the note **d**. The second chord is called *C major 7*, or $C^\triangle$.

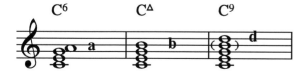

Let your ears decide what works and what not. We will look at the use of 6, major 7 and 9 notes in the Tunes section (page 37). In the II and V steps, you won't be using major 7s. These steps always feature *minor* 7s, as they are part of a cadence (see page 10). The minor 7s in Dm and G are **c** and **f** respectively:

Minor scales are less straightforward. There is more than one. As we saw last chapter, gypsy jazz mostly uses the *harmonic minor* scale. If you look at the minor Grappelli improvisation on page 42, you will notice this. Here is the A harmonic minor scale followed by Grappelli's notes on the tonic:

Check the beats and you will find only chord notes, with an added major 7 (**g♯**). Yes, the I in minor can have a major 7 just like the I in major! Try it on the piano.

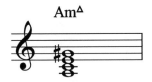

Minor Swing was recorded in the thirties. From the sixties onward, Grappelli often uses a slightly less gypsy scale, called *natural minor*, which doesn't use the **g♯**. Check it out, you are looking at the notes of C major again!

This scale works best on a downward phrase. You can even use natural minor on the V, which has a **g♯** in its chord. Try playing the following phrase over the V - it sounds great. The V resolves to a minor tonic, so it has a flat 9 (**f**) as well.

Use one scale for all the steps in a given key. In minor, you can choose between harmonic minor, with a major 7 (**g♯**) or natural minor, with a minor 7 (**g**). It depends on whether you want to sound gypsy or cool.

BASIC SKILLS

The following pages give an overview of techniques and exercises for a better understanding of Stéphane Grappelli's style. See them as building blocks which prepare you for the solos and chord changes that you will encounter in the Improvisation and Tunes sections.

You can use these exercises as a daily warmup before studying tunes. When you practice them, always start at a slow tempo. It is about control and precision, not speed.

Time

Swing is a difficult concept to understand, even when you have mastered it. A lot of players try to analyze it by writing it down. They represent the time of eighth notes (the basic note value in swing), either like this:

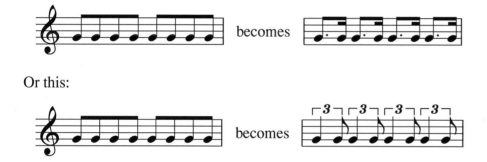

Now I want you to forget these notations. Don't try to interpret Swing. Just play your notes straight, like you would play J.S. Bach. That is the best approach for now.

You will start to swing naturally after you learn the different techniques in the following chapters. Good Bowing and Accents are the key, not the interpretations above.

Be aware that there is not one Swing feel. Every player has a personal style, but also, tunes and even phrases can have different feels. For example, a *run* (scale notes) will be more straight than an *arpeggio* (chord notes), which is more jumpy. Compare the following examples, they feel different.

listen to track 2

listen to track 3

Here are a few simple time exercises you can do without your instrument. Let's start by talking a walk. Take one step every two beats. There are four beats to the bar, so the steps are on one and three:

Add a finger click on the afterbeats, which are the second and fourth beats of the bar. Don't rush!

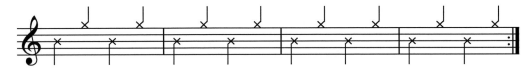

Snap the finger click with more energy, as if it has an accent. The two and four feel more important now:

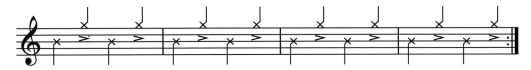

Stop walking and only click your energetic afterbeat-finger. If someone came in and heard your accents, they would think you were playing first and third beats. But keep playing them as afterbeats.

Let's walk a bass line. Walking bass lines are in four, so take one step to every beat:

Add your finger click on the *off-beats* (the 2nd, 4th etc. eighth notes in the bar). Keep it straight!

Now do these exercises while listening to a jazz tune. Make sure you start with a nice slow one. Imagine you are playing and communicating with the musicians - experience what happens if you slow down or speed up slightly. Then "lock in" with the band, walking and clicking totally in time.

Experience this feel when playing with the play-along tracks. Always have an ear open for the band. You will start to feel in command of Time - which is the essence of Swing.

The Grappelli Sound

This book is devoted to Stéphane Grappelli's hot jazz playing. He has charmed jazz, folk and classical audiences around the world with his elegant and romantic style. Grappelli's universal appeal came through the fact that he could make everyone feel as if he were playing for them alone.

A big part of this has to do with personality. Len Skeat, Grappelli's bass man for years, tells: "He could be angry about a certain thing only minutes before a concert, like telling one of the musicians off for being late or looking sloppy. Then as he went onstage he was completely transformed. All smiles, he played as sweet as ever. You would never have known what went on before."

Another part had to do with phrasing. Grappelli had a simple way of phrasing an improvised melody that was very close to the original melodic phrases of the composition. This makes even his most complicated runs and *licks* (bits of phrase) sound very natural, like someone talking or singing.

But before we go there, we will first analyze the violin techniques that create Stéphane's famous sound.

Accents and Ghost Notes

Creating a jazz sound has everything to do with highlighting certain notes and dropping others. It is like talking: you don't want to accent every word, it wouldn't sound natural. Good bowing control is essential to make these differences, which are called *articulation*, come out.

Here are some exercises to get the tone going. First of all, play light strokes and glue them together, so that you can hardly hear the bow changes. This is called *legato*:

Now add tiny accents at the start of every note, by pinching the index finger and thumb of your bow hand together. Release the tension immediately after playing an accent, and keep the legato feeling. Don't suddenly stop the bow on bow changes!

Let's introduce some rhythm. Glue consecutive eights together but make final eights short:

We now move the on-the-beat accents to off-beat notes. Notice that the accents were on *down* bows and are now on *up* bows.

listen to track 4

Always make sure you can hear a real difference between accented and non-accented notes. Contrast is what we need. To make the accents stick out even more, we have *ghost notes*. These are notes that are barely heard. Start by doubling the first exercise up, keeping the accents on the beat, and not losing the legato feel:

Now play the open d string on off-beat notes.

Try to lift the pressure on the d string notes, which means that the up bow is much softer than the down bow. Don't lose the on-the-beat accents! Exaggerate the effect so that you lose the off-beat notes nearly totally. You are now playing ghosted notes. It should sound like this:

sounds as

listen to track 5

There is another way of ghosting notes, which is a slurred version. First practice a non-legato or short version of our first exercise:

Now, in the same bowing add the notes on the d string without really playing them. It should sound the same - don't make the bowing longer, remember: *non-legato*.

listen to track 6

18

When all these bowing nuances are used together, the result is a very hot and active sound. The following Grappelli lick combines the two types of ghost notes with on- and off-beat accents, on a G chord.

listen to track 7

And here's another example, in the key of F, starting in third position and going down to first:

listen to track 8

Position Play and Open Strings

Violinist Eddie South, whose playing influenced the young Grappelli a lot, often stayed in third position for longer periods, ignoring possible open strings except with ghost notes. This gave his playing a more classical sound. The first eight bars of "Lady Be Good" played by Eddie South sound like this:

listen to track 9

Grappelli decided he wanted ease and speed, and so he always kept his fingering centered around the open strings, making use of them often. Look at his first eight of "Lady Be Good" and notice how he copies South's use of open string ghost notes, but starts in first position instead of third:

listen to track 10

19

When some extra *oomph* is needed (which was very often when playing with the Quintette of the Hot Club of France, featuring three loud guitars and bass), Grappelli goes up to third position and fifth position on the e string. Forget about the second or fourth positions as they will confuse your fingering:

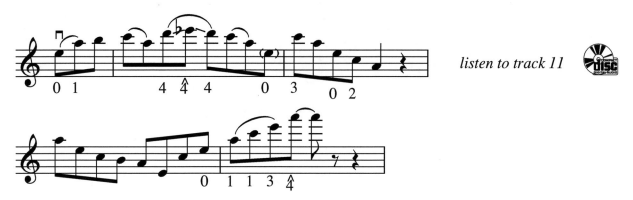

listen to track 11

Open strings play an important role in keeping the fingering simple and fast. When you play an open string, you are not using the fourth finger - saving a lot of time and energy! Try these two fingerings out.

A nice trick is combining an open string with the same note, fingered. This is a technique that Grappelli probably copied from guitarist Django Reinhardt, as Django also uses it often. Grappelli played it in third position, so let's do that too. Make sure you hit both strings together and don't lean too much on the open string.

The fourth finger can be used to play the semitone between third finger and open e string (**d♯** or **e♭**). This leaves the third finger available for the regular third finger note (**d**):

Using the positions in this simple way does put an extra demand on the bow: you will have to make more string changes. Practice the exercises in the chapters on Bowing (page 23) and Chord Practice (page 25) to develop flexibility and speed in your bowing hand.

Vibrato

When I wrote out my first Grappelli solo long ago, I was trying to get an effect that I considered a trill, to sound like the original and I couldn't get it. Later on, it turned out to be his vibrato!

The vibrato is wide and very fast. Your left hand won't be able to do it unless you exercise it. When you look at the vibrato movement, the finger goes up and down several times. I will call once up and down a *shake*. Let's start off with this lick, playing four slow shakes a note. Make the shapes really wide. Practice to a metronome speed of 50 for the half note, and repeat it on all the other strings.

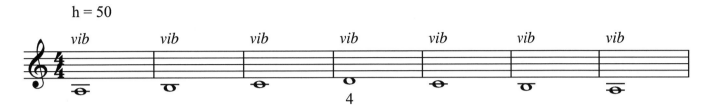

The trick is to play the shakes in time, as if they are notes themselves. Speed your vibrato up by playing more than 4 shakes per note (6, 8, ...) in the same metronome tempo. Keep the shakes going continuously: don't stop on note changes.

This way, develop a fast and wide vibrato, but don't use it on eighth notes. Listen to Grappelli's recordings and you will hear that he uses vibrato only on long notes, especially off-beat notes or phrase-final notes:

Vibrato is never used on a slide. Try it, it sounds comical. So whenever a slide occurs on a long note start the vibrato after the slide reaches its target note. This is for the real connoisseur - if you want, you can also decide that a slide rules out vibrato on that note.

listen to track 12

Harmonics

Grappelli was well-known for his use of *harmonics*. On every string, there is a range of possible harmonics. These are played by using a finger of the left hand but not pressing it down on the fingerboard. The finger just touches the string on the position where it would normally hit a note.

We will look at the most common harmonic positions. These divide the vibrating string in two, three or four. The examples are on the g string but apply equally to all other strings.

The first harmonic is a stretched fourth finger in third position on the g string, touching the location of the **g** octave. This gives us the same note, but with a different, breathy sound:

1st harmonic (1/2 string)   sounds as

The second harmonic is played in first position with the fourth finger (normally the **d**). The actual sound is this **d**, but an octave higher:

2nd harmonic (1/3 string)   sounds as

The third harmonic is played in first position with the third finger (normally the c). The actual sound is **g**, two octaves above the open string **g**:

3rd harmonic (1/4 string)   sounds as

Try these harmonics on the d, a and e strings as well. This system works on all strings.

The second and third harmonics have a kind of dominant-tonic relation (see the Chords chapter, page 11), which makes the combination an ideal ending to a phrase. Grappelli uses this often. The following example shows first the fingering and then what it should sound like:

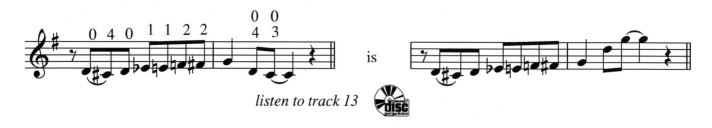

listen to track 13

This gimmick has become the theme of "Daphne" (page 49), a tune which was probably conceived in the studio as the Quintette were recording. Play the fingering - it is third position - and see what it should sound like.

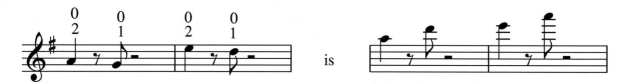

That's all for now - check out the Tunes section (page 37) to see how Stéphane Grappelli combines all the different techniques in this chapter. There you will also learn more about slides, pushes and pulls.

Bowing Exercises

Let's practice some bowings on the scale of G major. You can substitute the following examples with any other scale to get your fingers used to other keys - at the end of the Chord Practice chapter (page 29) you will find most common keys.

First see what happens when we try to fit a scale in the 4/4 bar. It finishes before the beat:

We want to make the scale more symmetrical, so that we can move up and down without losing the beat. The solution is to add one note to the scale. This extra note can be inserted in different places - we will add a **c♯** (sharp 4) going up and an **e♭** (flat 5) going down, to get a little closer to Grappelli's style:

Now we are ready for some practice. Here are some basic bowing exercises that you can use as a daily warmup, practicing speed, accents and tone. Repeat each example at a slow speed until you have really mastered it. Then take it a little faster. Practicing short intervals several times a week will yield better results than one long session. Use the metronome every now and then to check your time.

The first bowing is *straight bowing*. Remember I told you to play even eights, as you would play Bach. Don't try to swing, that comes later.

Adding slurs against the beat gives us a bowing I call *the chain*. This is not to be used all the time as it is too regular, but it is great in combination with other bowings:

Every slur should start with an accent. As you see, the accents are on off-beats because of the off-beat slurs. This is where swing starts to come in!

The straight and chain bowings combined can form all kinds of patterns. One very useful one is what I call the *jazz bowing*. It turns the bow round every half bar so make sure you learn it carefully, that you repeat it often enough to feel comfortable with it. And play those accents.

listen to track 14

Grappelli often uses a combination of three and two slurred notes, so here is how to practice that. Try to stay in the same part of the bow, by using a bit more bowing speed on the second slur of the bar:

Another Grappelli bowing looks like this:

Playing all these examples through, you will notice that you are always starting the bar with a *down* bow. This is a way of helping you "feel" the beginning of the bar without thinking too much about it.

Now, create your own bowings, combining straight notes and slurs of two or three notes. Make sure you don't start too many slurs on the beat - you need off-beat accents to swing. And try to get into a feel where the first beat of the bar is always on a down bow. Here is an example:

etc.

listen to track 15

You are improvising your own bowing rhythms! It takes some time to get used to this free bowing style. To create a steady time feel, tap your foot to accompany yourself or use the metronome as a beat. Start the slurs on different beats and off-beats, and don't forget to play accents.

Chord Practice

Chord playing on the violin takes the form of *arpeggios*. These consist of three or four notes, depending on the function of the chord. When we look at the root chord or first step chord of G, we see it has the three notes **g**, **b** and **d** in its arpeggio:

As with scale playing, an even number of notes is needed to fit the bar. With the three note arpeggio, as with the seven note scale, we add an extra note to make it regular.

This extra note, **e**, is the 6. As we saw on page 14, other possible additions to a chord are the major 7 (in this case **f♯**) and the 9 (**a**). That the **a** is called 9 and not 2, has to do with voicing. This gives us two more arpeggios on G:

Here is how to study repeated runs on one arpeggio. When you cross a string, make sure you change the angle of the bow as little as possible. Grappelli was famous for his economic use of the bow, both in the amount of bow length used and the small up and down movement of his bowing elbow.

As with the scales, get into a steady groove and don't try to play too fast in the beginning. Let your left hand become absolutely sure which fingers go where. Use the bowings and accents from last chapter on all the arpeggio exercises in this chapter. I have written the jazz bowing, but use other bowings as well. The large number of string changes involve quite a refined bowing hand so there is much to be learned:

listen to track 16

With the arpeggios on G, two complete octaves are played in first position all through. To do this with other keys that have their root note higher up on the violin, use a different arpeggio note to start on. Find their first chord note low on the G string. Let's look at Dm as a root chord, with an added 6. Starting on Dm's 5, the **a**, enables us to stay in first position all the way.

With this trick, you can now practice any chord arpeggio in two octaves, first position, using all the strings, with all kinds of bowings. Check out the arpeggio on F with an added 9:

And here is a minor arpeggio: Cm with a major 7.

Until now, we have only looked at tonic chords. In most tunes you will find minor 7 chords, dominant 7 chords and diminished chords. When you come across a new chord, check its notes and practice the arpeggios as above. Here are all three fingerings for the different diminished chords:

These fingerings are not only for G, G♯ and A diminished chords. The G fingering also holds for B♭, D♭ and E diminished as these are all a minor third apart and the notes are the same. Likewise, the G♯ fingering holds for B, D and F diminished and the A fingering is the same for C, E♭ and F♯ diminished.

The last arpeggio exercise is a really nice one for practicing chord sequences in tempo. Use only quarter notes and play arpeggios over the chords, following the chord changes. Try this on the chords to the Am improvisation (page 42). In minor, too, we can add the 6, major 7 or 9 notes to fill the bar:

There are a lot of jumps on chord changes. Solve this by moving to the closest note in the new arpeggio instead of jumping to its root. This changes the form of the arpeggios a bit:

It becomes even smoother when we fit in some scale bits. Use the harmonic minor scale of Am throughout, except on the Bb7 chord, where you play bb instead of b. Notice that ab is the same as g#.

And, to make it sound more like a walking bass line, add some chromatic leading notes. These notes are *sharp* scale or arpeggio notes when leading up to the next note, and *flat* when they lead down. Keep chord-friendly notes on the beats:

listen to track 17

28

Don't practice arpeggios in all keys. Gypsy jazz is violin friendly so you won't find a tune in, say, B major or D♭ minor. The best thing is to practice arpeggios as you encounter them in new tunes. Look at the chord sequence and isolate new chords that you haven't played before. Write their arpeggios out in the way you saw at the beginning of this chapter, starting on the g string and staying in first position. The first chord of "Sweet Georgia Brown" in F, for example, looks like this:

Below are the most common keys to Grappelli's tunes. I have written out the arpeggios with an added 9. Don't practice too long at a time but keep it short and often. And use those bowings!

29

IMPROVISATION

Working through the previous chapters, we have looked at chords, scales, bowings and the general Grappelli sound. Using these techniques, you can now step by step create your own swinging Gypsy Jazz solo.

The most important thing to remember if you haven't improvised before, is that it works like any other study: practice makes perfect. Don't expect to sound great straightaway. In fact, expect to annoy your neighbors at first. But realize that you are improvising on the hardest instrument there is - the fiddle!

Start with the examples and then gradually let go of the notes to find your own. Experience the joy of freedom on your instrument. Once you get into this feel, whatever level you are at, you will be able to play with any other jazz musician in the world as long as you agree on the song, tempo and key. Not bad, huh?

Staying on a Chord

We start on one chord, C major. No sharps, no flats. Use *playalong track 18: C major chord*. The tempo is nice and slow - pay attention to the count-in tempo. Take the time for each example until you feel you have tried all possibilities. Make your own bowings. First play the scale up and down as you like:

Now "break" the scale into bits, regular or irregular:

Play arpeggios the same way. Use the C^6 arpeggio which adds an **a** to the chord.

Start combining scales and arpeggios, using your own imagination:

You are already improvising! Here are some examples of *licks* that work very well on C major. Play a lick, wait, and play another one. Or a bit of scale. Or an arpeggio. And take time between these bits of music.

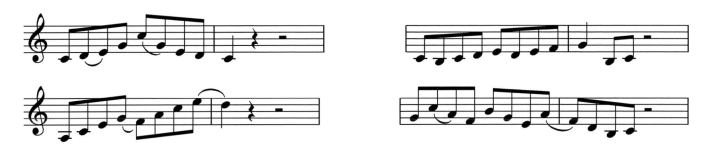

Taking time between different bits is called *phrasing*. Now use some open strings. Remember this one?

And maybe a little sliding and vibrato here and there:

Chromatics add a lot of spice to the sound. We saw on page 28 that you can use a sharp or flat note as a *leading note* towards a chord-friendly note.

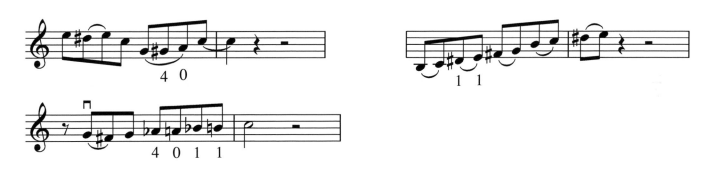

And it wouldn't be jazz without *syncopation*: make off-beat notes important, using accents:

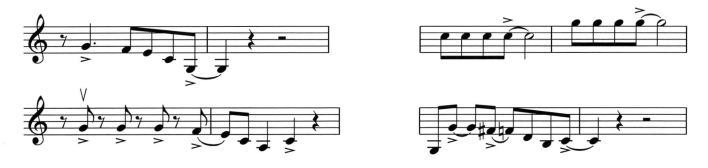

All these bits of solo you can transpose and practice on other solitary chords. Good ones are G, D, F and B♭. Check the scale for sharps and flats before you start.

Now, let's have a short run through a minor chord, Am. Go back to its harmonic minor scale:

Make yourself familiar with the scale the same way you did this on the C major chord, using scale and arpeggio bits and some bowings. *Use playalong track 19: A minor chord.*

Find Am's chord additions major 7 (**g♯**) and 9 (**b**) by looking at the scale. When you play the Am⁶ arpeggio, try using a major 6 (**f♯**) instead of the regular scale note (**f**). Major 6 on a minor chord is a useful sound.

Here are some specific A minor licks.

Some licks work equally well in major or minor:

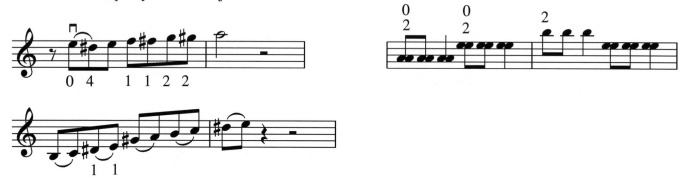

Practice this on Gm as well, or any other minor key you might acome across in a song. Put these licks in your 'bag' and then it's time to move onto the next step: *chord changes.*

32

Chord changes

The Blues

In the Scales chapter (page 14) we saw that in a given key, one scale works for all the steps. Now let's look at a 12 bar "Blues for Steff" in C, which has steps I, IV and V. V is the G^7 chord.

For the *head* or *theme*, I have chosen a melody that remains the same through the changes. Go ahead and play along with *track 20* of the CD. Use parts of the head as licks anywhere in your improv.

Remember the scale of C major? Try playing it over the chords while you are improvising. On the tonic, emphasize the C arpeggio. On F and G^7, use more of the F and G^7 arpeggios. Here are some examples:

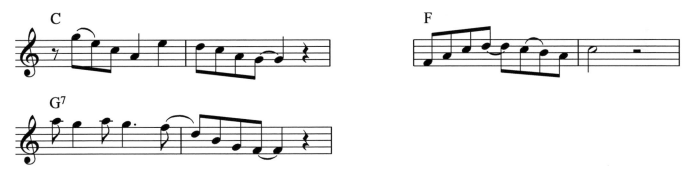

One chord needs a special treatment and that is C^7. The 7 of C dominant 7 is a **b♭**. During the C^7 bar, use this instead of **b**. Make a nice line leading into F. You can choose to use a **b♭** during the F bars as well - it is a matter of taste. As long as you return to the C major scale in bar 7.

Now divide the 12 bars into four-bar phrases, just like the head. Use these phrases to keep track of where you are: 3 phrases make up one chorus. And make nice gaps - they give you time to think ahead!

This symmetry is a bit boring. Try making your phrases shorter or longer, and pause in different places. Don't lose the four bar feel. Keep those gaps between phrases. And throw in some accents:

On a short song like this you normally play several choruses. Start a new phrase in the 12th bar if you want to play another chorus (see the examples above). When you are finished, make a neat ending and leave some space in the 12th bar for the next soloist to start early if he wants.

Play straight lines, make them swing with clear accents and your own mix of bowings. Lock in with the rhythm section and you are away! A sample solo is available on *track 27*.

The II-V-I

Here is a tune in G, built around II-V-I and V-I cadences. The form is 8 bars + 8 bars or A-A, 16 bars total. These are all diatonic (one-scale) chords in the scale of G major, except for the G^7 and $C\#^{o7}$.

Playalong track 21
Medium swing

Two Five Stomp

T. Kliphuis

Write the chorus, that is just the chords, on a piece of paper. Just barlines and chord names. Four bars a line. This is your route map. First, check the scale, which is G major (one sharp). Always do this before you start on a new tune. It 'sets' the fingers of your left hand in the correct position.

There are two ways to handle the II-V-I. The easiest way is to ignore the II and treat the II-V as one big V, just like the head or theme does. Let's try doing that.

The other way is to emphasize the II, by playing its arpeggio notes, and then arriving on the V:

35

With these two ways of playing over the II-V-I in your head, play along with *track 28* and make your own phrases. If you run out of ideas, listen to the sample solo (*track 28*) or find your favorite C major licks on page 32, then transpose them into G major. That is a fifth up, and don't forget the **f♯**. For instance:

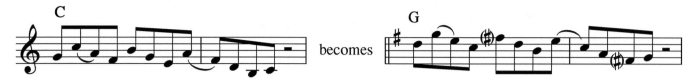

We now need to take a closer look at the two *non-diatonic* chords, G⁷ and C♯°⁷. They are not built up from only scale notes, like the other chords. They have the same function as we saw with C⁷ in "Blues for Steff" (page 33, bar 4): they lead into the next chord. In the G⁷ half bar, use the note **f** instead of **f♯**. Again, you can choose to keep the **f** on the C (IV) chord or to go back to the G major scale.

The C♯°⁷ chord is a diminished chord, which uses a different scale altogether. Here are the scale and the notes in the arpeggio. For the arpeggio's fingering, check the G°⁷ (=C♯°⁷) chord on page 27.

And here are some suggested licks on the C-C♯°⁷ bar:

Combine these bits of information to play a complete "Two Five Stomp" solo. Lock in with the rhythm section, and don't rush. You can even try playing a bit late, to make it sound more relaxed. Let your ears decide what is good Time feel. Play the gaps, use crisp accents and look for a combination of long and short notes.

You are now ready to deal with Stéphane Grappelli's notes. In the next section, his solos serve as a further introduction to leading notes, blue notes, and all the violin techniques that create the Grappelli sound.

TUNES

Here are six Stéphane Grappelli improvisations written out for you to study. They have been transcribed from recordings that are still accessible or have been re-released. Go on the net or order the recordings from your store - you need to hear what the transcriptions really sound like. I have tried to represent Grappelli's bowings and fingerings as accurately as possible, considering there is no visual material available of these tracks.

Playing level progresses with each following solo. The first three are based on the chord changes of a blues in C ("Viper's Dream"), on the Am changes of "Minor Swing" and the rhythm changes of "Daphne", which were all recorded in the thirties with Django Reinhardt and the Quintette of the Hot Club of France.

Then we skip a few decades and look at Grappelli's early seventies improvisations based on the changes of "I Can't Give You Anything But Love" and "Sweet Georgia Brown". The last example is his sweetest ballad chorus ever, on changes for Django's evergreen *Nuages*, in a lineup with Swiss guitarist, Pierre Cavalli.

With each tune, I first dicuss the form and some general aspects, then go on to examples of the techniques that we have been working on in this book. Use Grappelli's licks to enhance your Gypsy Jazz sound, but don't forget to make your own variations, lines and notes too. Practicing a solo is great, but when you are performing make sure you have something to say for yourself.

The playalong tracks 20 and 22-26 are there to learn the chord changes and improvise on them - your way! I have added some sample improvisations on these changes on tracks 27-33, just to give you an idea of some alternative lines.

Grappelli Improvisation No. 1

Playalong track 20
Medium swing

Grappelli improvisation based on the blues chords in "Viper's Dream".
Recorded 1937 - CD *Django Reinhardt Complete Vol. 6 - Swinging with Django* (Frémeaux)

Form

This is how the Quintette played the blues: they liked it *hot*. Hot means up-tempo and not too serious. The song "Viper's Dream" starts with a totally different head but the improvising is done on a blues chorus. Notice that the IV has an added 6, which is a regular gypsy jazz chord addition.

You are looking at a 24 bar solo over two 12-bar choruses. Write out the chords on a piece of paper like you did with "Two Five Stomp" (page 35). Use this to memorize the tune, as you shouldn't read melodies or chords on stage. Improvise on the "Blues in C" playalong track (*track 20*) and listen to the sample (*track 27*).

The 6

At the time of this recording, Grappelli used the 6 on nearly every chord, esp. I and IV. On C, the 6 is **a**:

On F^6, the 6 is **d**. This licks starts just like the first one in C, with a downward arpeggio:

The flat 3

A blues always has *blue notes*. The first blue note in any major key is the *flat 3*. When you play a flat 3, you are in fact playing a minor note over a major chord. This is a bluesy feel, which Grappelli likes to use a lot on the tonic (C). The flat 3 is **e♭**:

There aren't any IIs in this tune. Still, Grappelli plays over the V as if he were playing II, and it sounds great! The V is G⁷ and II would be Dm⁷. This trick of substituting a minor II for a major V works. Try it. For your understanding, compare Grappelli's lick to the notes of Dm⁷ below:

bar 21

Slides

Just playing the notes is not enough. You need to add your own interpretation of the sound, making it swing more. A very nice sound is the *slide*. The most common slide starts approximately a semitone below the target note and then pulls up. In this example, start the slide around **b** to end on the **c**:

bar 17

Start the slide on the beat, not before as the notation would suggest. Start loud and finish soft. We want to hear the slide, not the target, as our ear anticipates the target anyway. You can also use a slide to find a difficult high note, or a stretched position, as below:

bar 21

Downward slides are used to end a note, going down to roughly a semitone below the start note. As above, play the beginning louder than the end. You will often see a downward slide started with an accent:

bar 14

Here, the third finger slides down a semitone to its original (**d**) position and the second finger takes over.

This page has been left blank to avoid awkward page turns.

Grappelli Improvisation No. 2

Grappelli improvisation based on the chords in "Minor Swing".
Recorded 1937 - CD *Django Reinhardt Complete Vol. 6 - Swinging with Django* (Frémeaux)

Form

The solo transcribed here is from the famous first recording of "Minor Swing", in 1937. Grappelli really gets going on this one and plays four ripping choruses. Look at the sharps and flats: apart from some blue notes it is mostly the A minor harmonic scale with **g♯**. Play *track 29* to hear a sample.

The chorus is 16 bars (two times 8), where the steps go I-IV-V-I and IV-I-V-I. The B♭7 chord is a different way of playing the V, E7. The only change to the scale is that **b** becomes **b♭**. Have a go with the playalong track to familiarize yourself with the changes.

The pickup bar

In all the solos, you will notice Grappelli starts before the first bar. This is to connect his solo to the last notes of Djangos solo, which normally finishes early. That way, the music continues. We call this early start a *pickup*. Try it yourself, it works!

The #7

The minor scale has a major 7, **g♯**, as shown above. Grappelli skips that note when he plays the tonic:

bar 39

But uses it naturally on the dominant chord:

bar 21

The 6

If you look at all the IV chords (Dm) in the solo, you will see many **b**s played on this chord. On Dm, **b** is the 6. In fact, it is a major 6, as we have seen on page 32. Grappelli uses the 6 a lot, but particularly on minor subdominant chords, like the Dm. Here is an example. Try introducing the **b** on all Dm chords in your improvisation - it sounds much more interesting than before. Keep it!

bar 19

The dominant flat 9

When you look at this dominant chord, E⁷, you will find that Grappelli always adds the flat 9 (**f**) when he plays an arpeggio. In effect, he plays a flat nine dominant chord as discussed on page 12:

bar 6

He also combines the **e** and the **f** - listen to how this interval jars.

bar 37

The flat 5

We saw in the "Viper's Dream Blues" solo (page 38) that a blue note is a form of minor in major. So what do we do in a minor tune if we want that blue feeling? We suggest a kind of double-minor (which is diminished, in fact) by playing a flat 5. Am's flat 5 is e♭ and you can see it a lot in the solo. Here is an example:

bar 11

Pushes and pulls

The flat 5 blues sound is exaggerated by the use of *pushes* and *pulls*. A push takes the note up a half step, a pull takes it down. You use the same finger. Here is a push (1st finger) followed by a pull (3rd finger):

pickup bar

Lean on the bow a bit when you push or pull, don't try to hide the effect. As with slides, the most important part is the beginning. You can release the pressure on the target note. The combination of push-pull is very effective:

bar 14

45

Grappelli must have enjoyed the effect, and so do the band, for he keeps going for ever on this one:

bar 46

Vibrato

Practice a wide, fast vibrato as described on page 22. Use it on the longer notes and phrase final notes. With a really long note, it is a good idea to start the vibrato a little late:

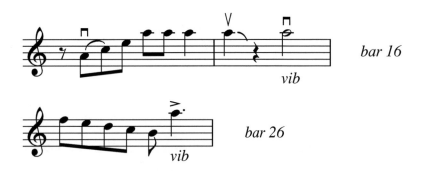

bar 16

bar 26

On final notes, Grappelli often uses a combination of vibrato and a down slide, which keeps the tension even though the phrase stops.

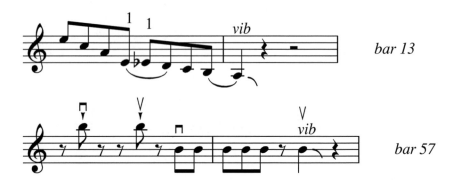

bar 13

bar 57

Here, play a short vibrato as if you are accenting the note, then drop the finger a semitone down and release it so that you hear the open string. All of this in the space of a quarter note - it sounds very hot!

Use the A minor licks from the Improvisation chapter (page 30) and combine them with what you see here. Make your own phrases. Try practicing a few Grappelli examples with his bowings, and then thinking up your own bowings. They should feel relaxed and fit your right arm technique. You are the boss.

Grappelli Improvisation No. 3

Playalong track 23
Medium swing

Grappelli Improvisation based on the chords in "Daphne".
Recorded 1938 - CD *Django Reinhardt Complete Vol. 7 - Christmas Swing* (Frémeaux)

Form

There are three Hot Club de France recordings of "Daphne". The first one has them playing with violinist Eddie South (1937) and the last one is from the Reinhardt/Grappelli Rome sessions in 1949. The one we want is the famous one from 1938, its theme played by Grappelli in harmonics (see page 22). Django takes the first two choruses and then Stéphane plays one chorus before concluding with the theme.

When you write out the chords, you will notice that the form is 32 bars, divided in four 8-bar blocks, where the third block is in a different key and all the other blocks are identical. We call this form AABA, where B is called the *middle eight* or *bridge*.

The majority of jazz tunes are in the 32-bar AABA form. Normally, however, the bridge will have a different chord sequence from the As. Here, it is the same, only a semitone up. The basis of this tune is the II-V-I. We have learned to play one scale over these chords. "Daphne" is in D major so that is the scale to use:

The key change on the bridge asks for a different scale, that of E♭ major. There is an abrupt change from D to E♭ on bar 17, which can be preceded by an upbeat (Grappelli's last two notes in bar 16, **d** and **e♭**, *anticipate* the new key). The last bar of the bridge, bar 24, is A⁷ which is in the key of D again. So we play the scale of E♭ in bars 17 through 23 only. Here are the notes. For a sample of these two keys, play *track 30*.

The II-V-I

In the Improvisation chapter you saw that playing the II-V-I meant either emphasizing the chord arpeggios or glossing over the chords using all scale notes. Here is an example of the first technique. On the Em⁷ (II) we find chord notes **b** and **g** on the beats, on A⁷ (V) we see **a** and **f♯** (the 6).

bar 2

In the bridge there is a good example of disregarding the steps and just playing a scale run. Of course, we are thinking in E♭ now - Fm⁷ is II and B♭⁷ is V:

bar 18

48

Bowing

Keep the bow on the string at all times. Use the upper half of the bow, from the middle upwards, but stay four inches from the tip. If you play the lower half of the bow it feels uncomfortable, and right at the tip you lose power.

When you practice this solo, stay on top of the beats. Feel the beat in your bowing hand - nearly every beginning of a bar is down bow. Try playing the suggested bowings, or if you find a bowing that suits you better: use that. I have added accents whenever Grappelli plays them, so let them come out. Don't lose the smooth, legato feel.

If you run into problems go back to the Accents and Bowing exercises on pages 17 and 23.

The 4

One note that is not chord-friendly (like the 6, major 7 or 9) is the 4. This note doesn't fit the chord at all, so when you play it as an independent note it sounds bad. Try it:

However, when you study the improvs in this book you will find many 4s on the beats, even first beats. The only reason the 4 sounds allright when Grappelli plays it, is because he uses it as a *leading* note: it resolves downward into the 3 (**g** to **f♯**):

bar 3

Or upwards to the 5, in a chromatic run (**g** to **g♯** to **a**):

bar 11

And here is an example on the A⁷ chord. The 4 is **d**, leading down to the 3 (**c♯**):

bar 7

In minor keys, the 4 is less of a problem. You can play it as a regular note as long as you don't overdo it. Check out the Am improvisation (page 42), bars 44 through 56, where the 4 in Am is **d**.

Chromatics

We have now discussed the 4 as a leading note. There are all kinds of possible leading notes, which as independent notes wouldn't sound right. Most of these are *chromatic* or non-scale notes. They give an extra color to a phrase. Have a look at this:

bar 21

If you check back to the E♭ scale on page 48, you will see that **f♯** and **b** are non-scale notes. These are used as leading notes for **g** and **c** respectively. Don't be confused by the notes in between. Here is a reduction:

Here is a nice chromatic leading note lick going up and down in the key of E♭: You can study this lick in any key, as long as you use chord notes for the target notes:

Here are some more chromatic licks, where Grappelli uses **g♯** on Em⁷ as a leading note to connect to A⁷:

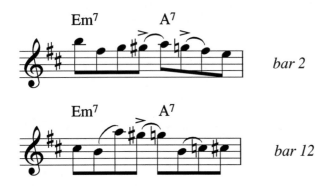

bar 2

bar 12

The diminished chord

In this recording, as in other early recordings, Grappelli is a bit sloppy with his approach to diminished chords. Going back to what we learned on page 36, and transposing that, G♯°⁷ should have the following scale:

At least we would expect a **g#** on the third and fourth beats, not a **g**. Grappelli just continues as if the whole bar is one big G chord, not G-G#°7: better not do this yourself, you won't get away with it.

bar 6

bar 14

The last time round, though, he does play the correct change. This lick has a rather tough fingering but can come in very handy:

bar 30

Anticipation

Grappelli is a master of anticipation. This means playing notes and licks of a chord that is still to come. Let's look at an example.

bar 31

Just looking at chord notes and basic rules, the **d** in the first bar is not correct. Our ears, however, tell us a different story. Expectation plays a major role in how we experience jazz improvisation. We expect a dominant 7 chord to resolve into its tonic. We expect II to lead to V. The experienced jazz player can play with this expectation and play certain lines early (anticipate).

bar 13

Here, Grappelli plays a dominant 7 note (c) on the first chord D, making it D⁷, and resolves this note into the **b**, which makes it sound as if we are already in a G chord (which is the next bar).

Grappelli Improvisation No. 4

Playalong track 24
Medium Swing

Grappelli improvisation based on the chords in "I Can't Give You Anything but Love".
Recorded Live 1971 - CD *Stéphane Grappelli - The Collection* (Castle / Sanctuary)

Form

This is a Grappelli improvisation recorded live in London, 1971, just before his solo career took off worldwide. His playing is fresh and it's the best tempo for this piece I have ever heard. He starts with a perfectly executed theme - check out the recording and compare this to a jazz singer like Ella Fitzgerald. At the end of the theme, he plays a long four-bar pickup into bar 1 of the improvisation, which is what we will be looking at.

The form is 32 bars, divided in two 16-bar parts. We call the two parts A and B. They both start the same: bars 1 through 4 equal bars 17 through 20. Make sure you know the difference and where it occurs (bar 21). The key is G major. You know the scale. For a sample solo, play *track 31*.

Harmony

Let's look at some new chords. Earlier on, I promised you the VI: here it is. The VI is Em⁷ and can be treated like the I (G). In fact, it includes the notes of G (g, b, d) and could also be written as G⁶. It adds some extra direction to the II-V-I cadence because of the relation between VI and II. The complete cadence is VI-II-V-I. As it is a diatonic chord, you use the notes of the tonic scale just like on the other steps. In short, don't pay too much attention to the VI, just play.

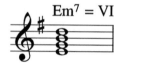

The VI is also used in a dominant way, as a preparation for the last II-V-I cadence in the piece (bar 28). E⁷ is not a diatonic chord, and instead of a **g** use the note **g♯** in that bar:

And then there is the dominant II, where we use **c♯** instead of **c**:

bar 13

Remember how to play over a dominant? If not, check the explanation in the Blues on page 33.

Articulation

This solo is a good example how carefully Grappelli articulates his notes. I have annotated as much as possible the different dots, dashes, and accents. You can find explanations of these articulations in the Grappelli Sound chapter (page 17).

As a general rule, consecutive eighth notes are always legato, or connected together. Never try to make them short, just play them as they come:

bar 23

Consecutive quarter notes, when not emphasized, will normally be short:

bar 39

Grappelli likes to contrast this with phrases of long quarter notes, which sound more suave:

bar 14

One stock phrase of his is a quarter note followed by two eights, where the quarter note is always long, and often has quite a lot of vibrato added to it:

bar 37

The following bar from the end is a bit like this, with long, higlighted first and third beats and short (softer) second and fourth beat quarter notes.

bar 59

Slurred ghost notes

In the Grappelli Sound chapter (page 17), we looked at the effects of ghost note playing. Here is the second kind, which has a slurred bowing. The second, fourth, etc. eighth notes are hardly played, because the bow accents the start and whispers the end of every slur. You should hardly hear the open string **d**, but because it is there it adds to the excitement. Try it.

bar 5

The 9

Grappelli uses the 9 mostly on dominant 7 chords. It is a chord-friendly note which 'opens' up the chord. Here are some examples on G⁷, where the 9 is **a**; and D⁷, where it is **e**.

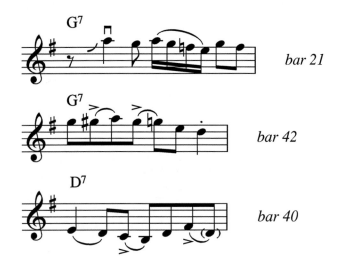

bar 21

bar 42

bar 40

The flat 3

We return to Grappelli's favorite blue note: minor 3 on a major chord. He used this more and more in his later years; we don't hear it so much in his pre-war period. A thing to know about the flat 3 is that used sparingly, it is great. But when you use it all the time, it is too much. As always, taste is very important. Stéphane Grappelli manages to stay just on the right side of the line.

On the tonic, check out these two flat 3 licks (**b♭**):

bar 37

bar 17

Normally the flat 3 is not used on dominant chords, as it is a leading note into their tonic (the 3 of V leads into the root of I). There is an exception: when you *alter* a dominant chord in a bebop way, there is such a thing as a *sharp 9*, which in fact is just a flat 3. Grappelli somehow combines bebop and swing notes on the dominants and gets away with it!

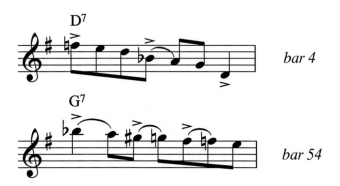

bar 4

bar 54

56

Slides

This solo is a case study in slides. Check back to page 40 to see how they are executed. More than before, as we are looking at the later Grappelli, it is important to play the beginning of a slide loud and the end soft. The distance between beginning and end is always roughly a semitone.

Emphasize the beginning of the slide so that you hear a very obvious **d♯** (semitone below **e**). The note's duration is three eighth notes. Start the slide exactly on the second eighth of the bar, not before. Arrive at the **e** on the third eighth note and the timing will be about right.

bar 9

Look at this example and try to play the different slides: up to a note, upwards after a note, and finally downwards after a note, which is called a *fall*.

bar 13

Theoretically, there is a fourth slide which lands on a note from above, but I haven't ever come across it in this style of jazz.

Harmonics

The last bar has the dominant-tonic harmonics as discussed on page 22. Make sure you don't press down the fingers of the left hand too much. Also, use a high bowing speed with little right-hand pressure.

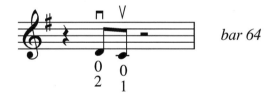

bar 64

There is a different use of the harmonic, which I would classify as 'noise', where after playing a regular note the left hand finger is released. This only happens to third position, first or second finger notes. The result is a whistling sound at the end of the note. See if you like it - it's a neat little effect: on the first note **e**, lift the second finger at the end.

bar 27

Grappelli Improvisation No. 5

Playalong track 25
Up-tempo swing

Grappelli improvisation based on the chords in "Sweet Georgia Brown".
Recorded Live 1971 - CD *Stéphane Grappelli - The Collection* (Castle / Sanctuary)

Form

Here is another vintage Grappelli solo from the 1971 Live in London concert, which has featured on many different collection CDs - check the album below to see where it is available now. After stating the head he launches into an improvisation with some chops, some characteristic third position licks and a lot of arpeggio playing.

The form, as with the chords of "I Can't Give You ..." (page 54), is AB, making up a total of 32 bars. B differs from A in bar 25 (Dm instead of C^7). Write out the chords: the key is F. Here is the scale:

For a sample solo, play *track 32*. On page 54, we encountered the VI for the first time. It reappears here, but not always as we would expect. The VI in F is Dm, but it has been changed into a dominant chord (D^7) in bars 1-4, 17-20 and 30 of the chorus. D^7 is not a diatonic chord, which you can see by the number of **f♯**s and **b**s that do not belong to the scale of F (bars 1-4, for example).

The same has happened to the II (Gm). We encounter a dominant II (G^7) in bars 5-8 and 21-24. There is also a regular or diatonic II in bar 31 (Gm^7).

Here are the D^7 chord and its scale (it is the same as scale of G, by the way, which is D^7's tonic chord):

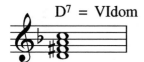

And here are the G7 chord and its scale (which is the scale of C - no sharps or flats).

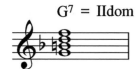

This looks very difficult, but using your ears will get you quite a long way. It does help to practice D7 going to G (a regular V-I in G major) and G7 going to C (V-I in C major).

There is one other chord, A7, which could be described as a dominant III, which I will not go into now. You can ignore it and just stay in F (bars 13-16) or Dm (bars 25-28). Check Grappelli's notes in these bars to see how he does this.

Phrasing

When you look at the first 16 bars of this solo, you will see that Grappelli plays a lot of four-bar phrases. At the end of such a phrase, he either plays a long note (bars 8, 12 and 16) or a small gap (bar 4). Notice that it is possible to have a short gap in the middle of a phrase, as in bar 7, without ending it.

Bars 17 through 32 are like a buildup, where the phrases become gradually longer. First two bars (17-18 and 19-20), then four bars (21-24) and finally eight bars (25-32, with a pickup on the last two notes of 24).

A characteristic Grappelli phrase start is a long note after the first beat, followed by lots of shorter notes. This solo has loads of them (all starting with a bown bow, by the way):

bar 5

bar 21

bar 61

Another way to start a phrase is by playing a pickup bar or a short pickup:

pickup bar

bar 24

When you end a phrase, make it sound logical, as if you are talking. On spoken sentences with a question mark, the pitch goes *up*. This phrase sounds like a question, asking for a reply:

bar 53

On spoken sentences with a final stop, the pitch goes *down*. This phrase sounds like a conclusion:

bar 63

Grappelli's music became so popular exactly because the phrasing is so natural. It feels as if he is talking to you directly. This is a characteristic of all good music and is worth remembering on stage. Try his various phrase lengths (two bars, four bars, eight bars), starts and endings yourself - find out where in the song they make sense to you and where they don't.

Bowings

Stylistically, the first three solos in this book are different from the last three in several respects. One of the big differences is bowing. In his later period, Grappelli uses shorter and fewer slurs, which means there is more room for accents and ghost notes than before. Contrast this old-style lick from the "Viper's Dream Blues" (page 38, bar 21):

With the modern bowings on this "Sweet Georgia Brown" lick:

bar 41

Let's see what this lick would have looked like with the old-fashioned 30s slurs:

From the seventies onward, the old-style feel of slurring up to 6 notes together has disappeared. Detached notes have now become the norm, with strategically placed slurs to ensure a smooth bowing feel, more accents and lots of ghost notes (see below).

Bowed ghost notes

I pointed out the use of the slurred ghost notes on page 55. Now it's time to look at bowed or detached ghost notes, where there are no slurs. Ghost notes can be played on up or down bows. Often, the ghosted note will be an open string, or two, as in the following examples:

bar 19

bar 22

But it is also possible to play fingered ghost notes - in case you think it is a waste of energy to play a note with your left hand and then ghost it, be aware that the ear does pick up these notes. It is worth the effort and boy, does it swing!

bar 42

The dominant flat 9

In his later days, Grappelli started to use the dominant flat 9 in major as well as minor. For the minor version, check out the first example on page 45. The dominant 7 chord in minor automatically has a flat 9 because of the harmonic minor scale.

In major, we can play the flat 9 but it is an *alteration*. It is a non-scale note. The V in F is C^7. Its flat 9 is **d♭**. Check out the following C^7 bar:

bar 43

You can play flat 9 on any dominant chord. It is a special color. As we saw on page 64, dominant VI (D^7) and dominant II (G^7) have their own scales. Try playing these but with a flat 9. On D^7, play **e♭** instead of **e**:

And on G^7, play **a♭** instead of **a**:

The third position

Check out the fingering of the following lick. Grappelli uses it a lot, always on Dm (or G^7, which uses the same chord-friendly notes):

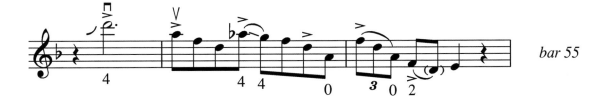

bar 55

The open a string is used to switch between first and third positions. Here is the lick the other way round.

The same open a string third position change applies to the chord F, where Grappelli plays this lick:

bar 61

Notice that he uses the third position first finger on the a string (**d**) in Dm as well as F. In fact, these chords are very alike so the licks are nearly interchangeable. Keep these fingerings, you will be able to use them a lot. Dm and F are very common chords in the keys that we play in.

Chops

You don't hear the chopping technique very much. When it is used it creates a nice change from the on-the-string legato feel that I am always talking about. Use the lower part of the bow, near the frog, and hit the string from the air, creating a very short attack. Practice up and down bows.

Here are two examples, the first one has double stops. Listen to the recording and try to copy the sound.

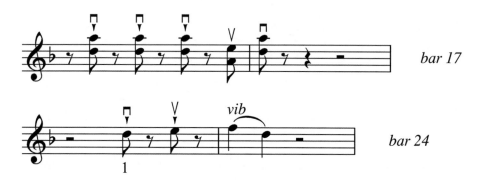

bar 17

bar 24

This page has been left blank to avoid awkward page turns.

Grappelli Improvisation No. 6

Playalong track 26
Medium ballad

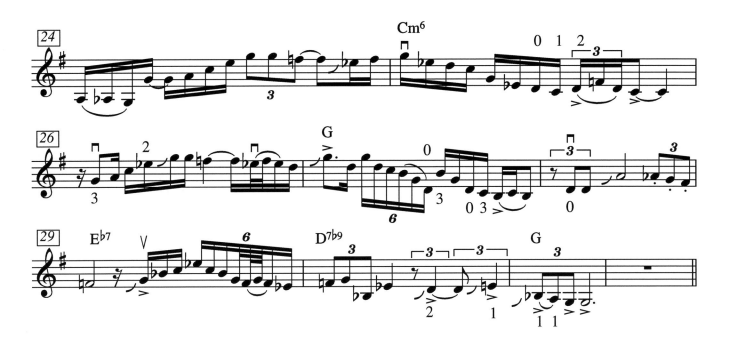

Grappelli improvisation based on the chords in "Nuages".
Recorded 1962 - CD *Stéphane Grappelli - Violin Jazz Master* (Tomato Music)

Form

This is a classic example of a Stéphane Grappelli ballad improvisation. His melodic lines on the chords of "Nuages" are tastefully accompanied by guitarist Pierre Cavalli. The difficulty of this solo may be over your head, but I have included it in this book to make some general observations about ballad playing.

Find the recording. Reading these notes without Grappelli's nuances, dynamics and free timing doesn't make sense. The form is AB once again - 32 bars total. Key of G. For a sample solo, play *track 33*.

Harmony

Let's look at the harmony in terms of steps. Bars 1-4 and 5-8 are II-V-I cadences in G (the tonic), where $E\flat^7$ is a dominant alternative for Am^7, the regular II.

Bars 9-16 are one big III-VI-II-V cadence that doesn't resolve into the I, and where III and II are dominant instead of minor.

Bars 17-20 are the same as before, and bars 21-24 are a modified II-V-I cadence in C (the subdominant).

Bar 25 has a Cm^6 chord. This lovely chord is the minor subdominant (or minor IV). It has a cadence function, IV-I (remember the blues?) which brings us back to G. Bars 29-32 feature the modified II-V-I again.

Notice that there are two dominant chords with a flat 9 (bars 2 and 22) that go to a major chord all the same. The flat 9s have been added because these notes are in the melody - this gives the piece its haunting character.

Time

When you listen to the recording and read what I have transcribed, you will see that it is only a rough representation of how Grappelli times the notes. He plays in so-called *rubato* style, which means playing very freely. This special, relaxed way of timing works only in a ballad.

Basically, the first beats of the bar are always in time:

pickup bar

The third beats, which are the middle of the bar, are often in time, but not always. Here is an example of a third beat which is played a little late - The next bar, however, starts exactly on time:

bar 12

Generally, Grappelli starts his phrases a bit slow, and catches up during the phrase (the end is a bit too fast, to compensate). This is real *rubato* (stealing) because you take some extra time first and give it back later.

bar 6

Grappelli never plays a melody the same way twice. He always finds yet another way to phrase it. Consider the tune's original pickup bar:

And see here his various alternatives, some early, some late, the last one with some short strokes, but always landing on the **f** in time:

pickup bar

bar 4

bar 16

bar 28

The minor IV

The Cm^6 chord is not a normal IV. That would have been C major. It is the minor IV, which is often used in ballads as an alternative to the V. The way we are now going to look at Cm^6 holds for any IV minor chord with a major 6. Here are the chord and its scale:

It is the scale of G (the tonic) with two exceptions: **e♭** and **f**. A trick that I use sometimes when going from IV minor to I is to play only the notes they have in common. Look at the scale of Cm⁶. The notes from **g** to **d** all belong to the scale of G as well. Try it yourself:

Grappelli uses another trick. On the Cm⁶ chord he plays some **f**s, which are strictly speaking not chord-friendly notes. Still, using an **f** makes the chord sound more like F⁷, which is a possible alternative to Cm⁶. Check it out, there is a big overlap.

bar 25

Soft touch

When you are playing a ballad, find a sweeter tone. Make the accents less heavy and use a more continuous vibrato, not too fast. The last thing you want to do is play too many notes. Keep aiming for natural-sounding phrases and even if you manage to be flexible with the time, stay true to those first beats of the bar.

Here is one bit of advice which I keep hearing from all the great jazz players that I meet: play the melody! Everybody loves hearing a good melody and as far as the tunes in this book go, you can't get much better.

That's all folks

This concludes the discussion of Grappelli's improvisation and style. Use certain bits of the book that you enjoy, to raise your general level. Then, as I said in the introduction, it's very important to play with real people. If you don't have a band yet, go and find one. Good luck!

DISCOGRAPHY

Here are some CDs that are well worth listening to. I have included introductions to Eddie South, Joe Venuti, Svend Asmussen and Stuff Smith as they all influenced Stéphane Grappelli at one time or other. Together these violinists represent the best on swing jazz fiddle ever.

The albums are presented in the order of their recording date. All of these recordings have been re-issued, compiled, and bought over by new labels. Quite a few can be found under various names, but I have tried to give you the easiest available issues.

Eddie South - Black Gypsy
1927-1941
Frog UK (2000)

The Chronological Joe Venuti
1928-1930
Classics Records 1246 (2002)

Django Reinhardt Complete - Vol. 6 and 7
1937-1938
Frémeaux (2002)

Stéphane Grappelli - Improvisations
Recorded Paris, 1956
Jazz in Paris series, Gitanes Jazz (2000)

Stuff Smith, Dizzy Gillespie and Oscar Peterson
Recorded 1957
Verve (1994)

Stéphane Grappelli - Violin Jazz Master
Recorded Paris, 1962
Tomato Music (2005)

Svend Asmussen and Stéphane Grappelli - Two of a Kind
Recorded Copenhagen, 1965
Storyville (2004)

Stéphane Grappelli - The Collection
Recorded London, 1971 (partly live)
Castle / Sanctuary (2005)

Oscar Peterson - Stéphane Grappelli Quartet
Vol. 1 and 2
Recorded Paris, 1973
Jazz in Paris series, Gitanes Jazz (2000)

Stéphane Grappelli, Joe Pass, NHOP
Recorded Copenhagen, 1979 (live)
Concord Jazz (2001)

Stéphane Grappelli - Vintage Grappelli
Recorded San Francisco, 1981
Concord Jazz (1991)

Stéphane Grappelli - Martin Taylor - Reunion
Recorded Scotland, 1993
Linn Records (1997)

Stéphane Grappelli - Live at the Blue Note
Recorded New York, 1996
Telarc Jazz (1996)

BIBLIOGRAPHY

Here are two jazz violin books that I read before writing this one. The Matt Glaser book features transcribed Grappelli solos and an interview with Grappelli about his thoughts on music. The Martin Norgaard book is a good introduction to mainstream and bebop playing on the violin.

Matt Glaser & Stéphane Grappelli - Jazz Violin
Oak Publications, New York (1981)

Martin Norgaard - Jazz Fiddle Wizard
Mel Bay Publications, Pacific (2000)

INDEX

Here is a summary of the main terms and techniques and the pages where they are explained: